Educational Worksheets for Children (Ordering concepts: Near and far depth perception)

This book contains 30 full color activity sheets for children aged 4 to 5

The web addresses for the 11 PDF books included under the special offer are shown below. We give permission for these books to be printed for personal use.

https://www.westsuffolkcbt.net/product/adding-easy/

https://www.westsuffolkcbt.net/product/kindergarten-math-2/

https://www.westsuffolkcbt.net/product/kindergarten-math-3/

https://www.westsuffolkcbt.net/product/kindergarten-math-4/

https://www.westsuffolkcbt.net/product/kindergarten-math-5/

https://www.westsuffolkcbt.net/product/kindergarten-math-6/

https://www.westsuffolkcbt.net/product/kindergarten-math-7/

https://www.westsuffolkcbt.net/product/kindergarten-math-8/

https://www.westsuffolkcbt.net/product/kindergarten-math-9/

https://www.westsuffolkcbt.net/product/1/

https://www.westsuffolkcbt.net/product/16/

The password is located on page 12 - at the bottom of the page

Which is the nearest? ☐

Which is the furthest? ☐

Which is the nearest?

Which is the furthest?

Which is the nearest?

Which is the furthest?

Which is the nearest?

Which is the furthest?

Which is the nearest?

Which is the furthest?

Which is the nearest?

Which is the furthest?

Which is the nearest?

Which is the furthest?

Which is the nearest?

Which is the furthest?

Which is the nearest?

Which is the furthest?

Which is the nearest?

Which is the furthest?

Which is the nearest?

Which is the furthest?

Which is the nearest?

Which is the furthest?

Which is the nearest?

Which is the furthest?

Which is the nearest?

Which is the furthest?

Which is the nearest?

Which is the furthest?

Which is the nearest?

Which is the furthest?

Which is the nearest?

Which is the furthest?

Which is the nearest?

Which is the furthest?

Which is the nearest?

Which is the furthest?

Which is the nearest?

Which is the furthest?

Which is the nearest?

Which is the furthest?

Which is the nearest?

Which is the furthest?

Which is the nearest?

Which is the furthest?

Which is the nearest?

Which is the furthest?

Which is the nearest?

Which is the furthest?

Which is the nearest?

Which is the furthest?

Which is the nearest?

Which is the furthest?

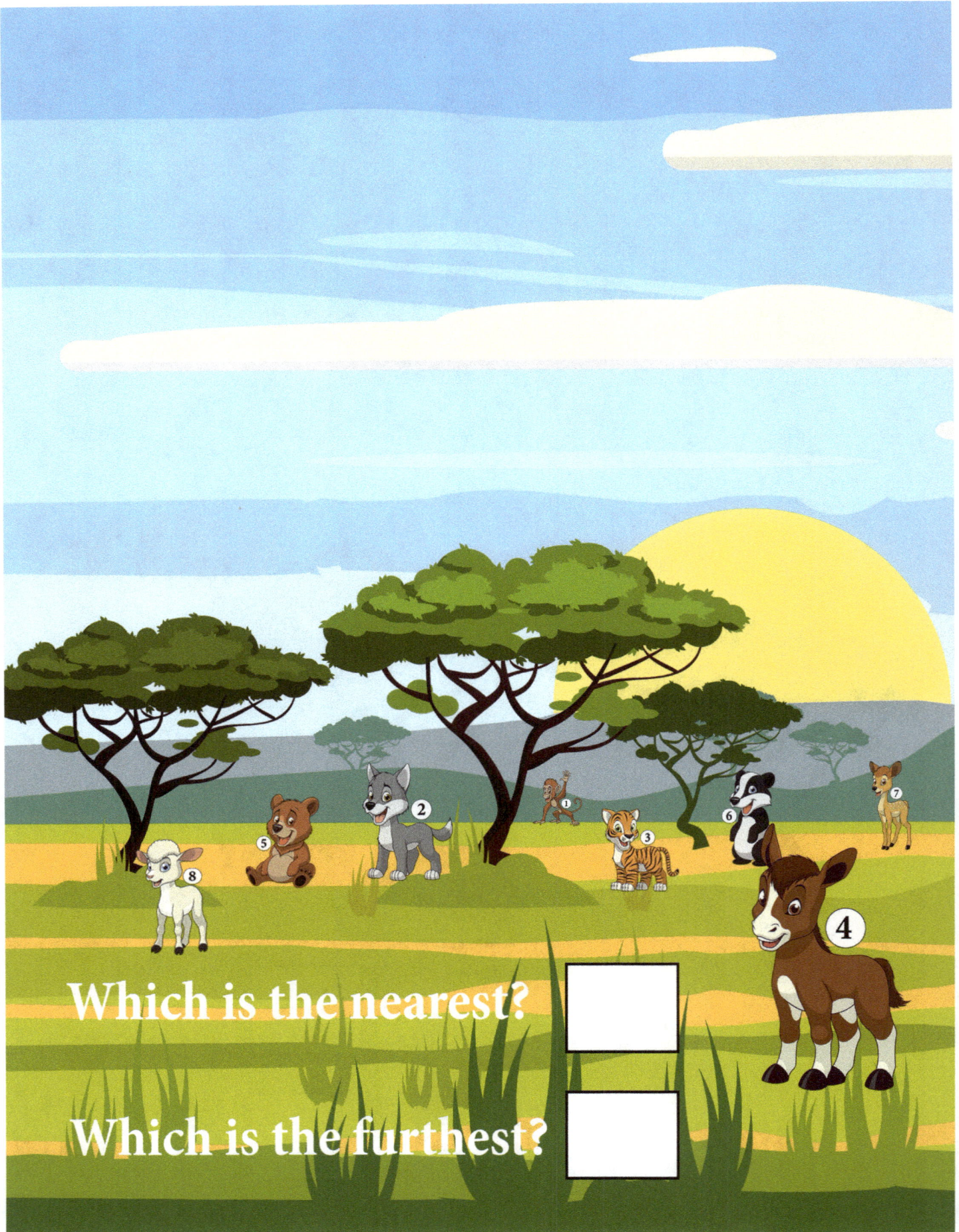

Which is the nearest?

Which is the furthest?

Which is the nearest?

Which is the furthest?

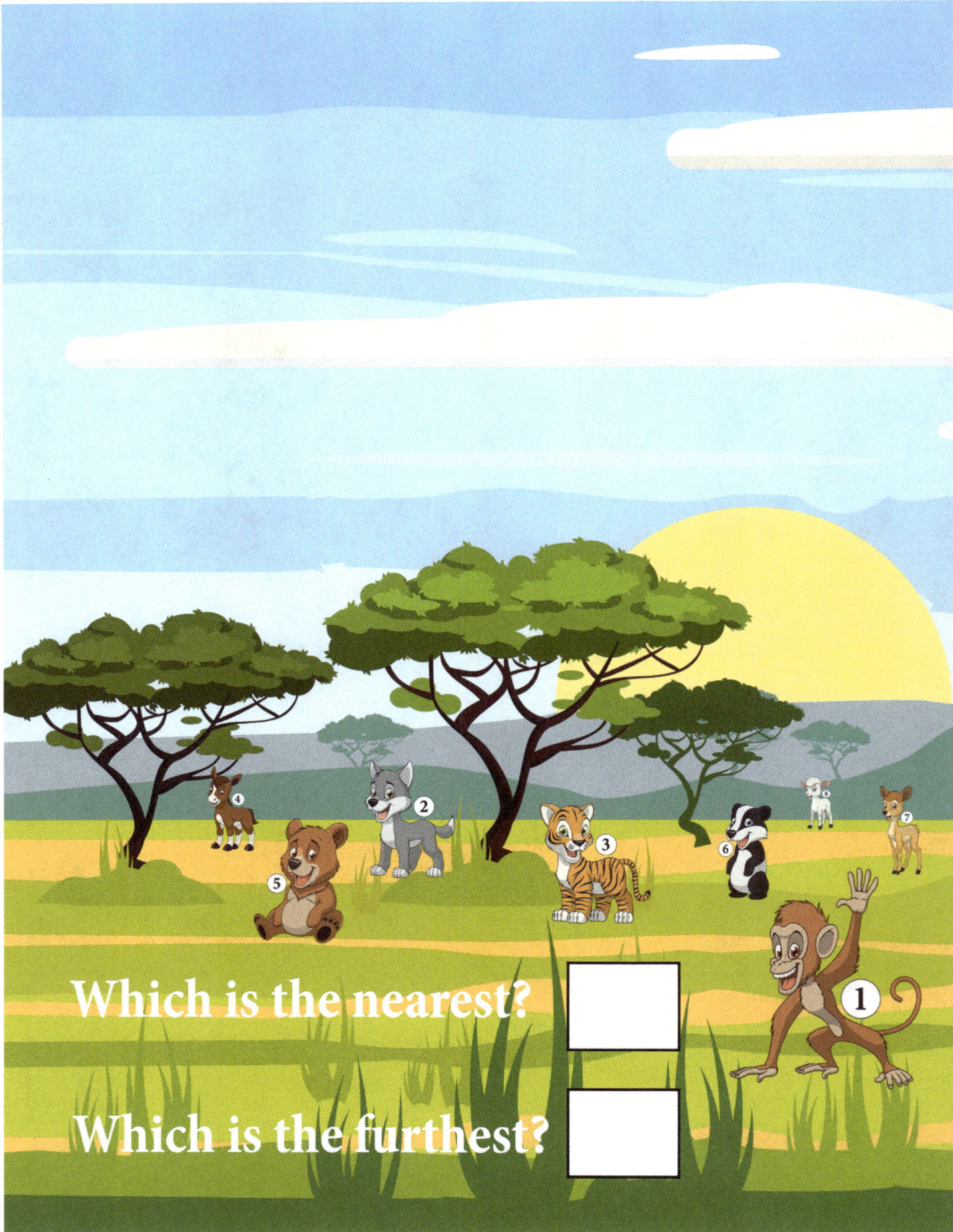

Which is the nearest?

Which is the furthest?

CPSIA information can be obtained
at www.ICGtesting.com
Printed in the USA
BVHW011411210819
556236BV00038BA/471/P